Pain & Joy in School *

Edward W. Schultz
Charles Heuchert
Susan M. Stampf

Introduction by
Matt Trippe

Research Press
2612 North Mattis * Champaign, Illinois 61820

ISBN 0-87822-048-8

Second printing 1974

 Illustrated by Marsha Ludlam

To Children:

*may they experience
less pain and more joy in school.*

Authors' Note

We thank the children and adults who have assisted us by telling their stories of Pain and Joy in School. They deeply care about children and the process we call education. We have faith that these experiences, shared with us, and now with others, will not be wasted. Children will experience more Joy and less Pain in School.

Contents

About School

He always wanted to explain things,
but no one cared.
So he drew.

Sometimes he would just draw
and it wasn't anything.
He wanted to carve it in stone
or write it in the sky.
He would lie out in the grass and look up in the sky
and it would be only the sky
and the things inside him that needed saying.

And it was after that that he drew the picture.
It was a beautiful picture.
He kept it under his pillow
and would let no one see it.
And he would look at it every night
and think about it.
And it was all of him and he loved it.

When he started school he brought it with him.
Not to show anyone, but just to have it with him
like a friend.

It was funny about school.
He sat in a square brown desk
like all the other square brown desks
and he thought it would be red.
And his room was a square brown room
like all the other rooms.
And it was tight and close. And stiff.

He hated to hold the pencil and chalk,
with his arm stiff and his feet flat on the floor, stiff,
with the teacher watching and watching.

The teacher came and spoke to him.
She told him to wear a tie like all the other boys.
He said he didn't like them
and she said it didn't matter.
After that he drew. And he drew all yellow
and it was the way he felt about morning.
And it was beautiful.

The teacher came and smiled at him.
"What's this?" she said.
"Why don't you draw something
like Ken's drawing?
Isn't it beautiful?"
After that his mother bought him a tie
and he always drew airplanes and rockets
like everyone else.

And he threw the old picture away.

And when he lay out alone looking at the sky,
it was big and blue, and all of everything,
but he wasn't anymore.

He was square and brown inside
and his hands were stiff.
And he was like everyone else.
All the things inside him that needed saying
didn't need it anymore.

It had stopped pushing. It was crushed.
Stiff.
Like everything else.

This poem was handed to a high school English teacher
the day before the writer committed suicide.

—Original source unknown   vii

Introduction

Man chooses the problems he is willing to live with as much as he chooses the goals he seeks to attain. Every solution has within it its own problems and our professional lives are presently captive of inescapable consequences of conditions which exist in school and society today. These circumstances of school and life include:

The failure of schools to serve responsibly in excess of 25% of the children delivered to it for present and future benefit

The heartless bureaucracy of too many schools, the depersonalization and inhumanity, and the delusions of helpfulness of too many teachers

The critical crises in mental health of our young particularly but of all ages really from early childhood through senior citizenry

Dropouts, pushouts, the unemployed, and the underemployed

An adult electorate that is anti-intellectual and doesn't read

Social crises of violence, crime, drugs and racism

Social stratification (in what is touted as an open, democratic society) based on intellectual fascism and promoted by schools through their pursuit of excellence to the exclusion of competence

These are some of the problems that stem largely from school practices that give lip service to the education of the whole child while personnel and resources are mobilized to promote scholarship and excellence in a few to the exclusion of concern for broadly based competence among the many. The U. S. Commissioner of Education, September, 1969 proposed the right to read as fundamental as the right to life, liberty and the pursuit of happiness. He announced that the achievement of this goal is education's moonshot for the Seventies. By the end of the present decade, no one should be leaving our schools without the skill and the desire necessary to read to the full limits of his capability. He was aware of the problems that stem from education's solutions when he observed that education has been a failure for the difficult more than 25% and that they stand as a reproach to all of us who hold in our hands the shaping of the opportunity for education. We all certainly share his concern but his solution is another matter. *The Right to Read—Target for the 70's* borrows its punch from the space program without cautioning that the success of NASA as well as the panic in educational circles created by the launching of Sputnik were both based on a commitment to develop excellence. After all, how many astronauts do we need? The Right to Read, however, is a program for universal competence. To move on it with manned space tactics is to doom it to failure as surely as compensatory and remedial programs have already failed. Reading, we know, is an essentially human activity as much as it is a specific skill. School practices which utilize needless competition and establish arbitrary standards that produce failures which then require remedial efforts are a much greater problem than the lack of specific skill on the part of the teacher in reading instruction. Love too is an essentially human endeavor as we all know, but few of us would hold much hope for its promotion through sex manuals.

To be fully alive, one must feel good about himself, solve problems rationally and be compassionate of others. If schools were fiercely dedicated to fostering joy, rational inquiry and human understanding, the present problems existent in the mainstream of education would dissolve considerably. Schools, however, only acknowledge developing the mind as their real responsibility regardless of the rhetoric in charters and journals. If they were more forthright, the situation would not be as bad. If they were to say that they care only about the head and can do nothing for the heart or the soul, then we'd have to deal with it. But to accept the challenge on the one hand and deny it on the other serves only to generate false complacency. Time is running out and we remain complacent at our peril. Concern for the head and failure to nourish the heart and the soul is a solution whose price we cannot afford. Joy and compassion are as necessary in humans as is reason. Advances in technology may come about largely through the exercise of reason but the use to which these advances are put—either for the benefit of mankind or for its destruction—are determined largely by the feelings we have about ourselves and our feelings about others. Feeling and doing are as important as thinking and remembering although what one observes in schools would suggest otherwise. The body and the spirit are as much to be celebrated as the mind. With the decline in influence of the church and the home, efforts in these areas by the schools are vital to our survival.

While medicine attempts cures of the ills of the body and the self to restore them to normality, the human potential movement tries to turn man on to the heights of creativity and fulfillment. Pupils at increasingly younger ages are showing through protest and unrest their responses to arbitrary controls and demands exercised by the schools.

Sadly, even the most able students are alienated and in many quarters the search goes on for alternatives to education. Choice has become possible with the development of free or open schools across the land. Through social welfare, we atone for man's initial inhumanity. This initial inhumanity in the circumstances of our lives is prompting many to drop out and seek fulfillment in isolation or communal societies.

Clearly, the schooling we need is not to learn our place in society nor to bow down to the demands of the technology and superstate. Rather, we need:

1. to discover joy through a variety of experiences that produce mastery and self discovery
2. to discover truth, reason and rational problem solving from the interrelatedness of knowledge and the integrated curriculum
3. to discover compassion through cooperative, helpful experiences with others that reduce our fears and broaden our understandings

Love of life, pursuit of truth and human compassion demand that we each in our own way be adamant in our refusal to participate in the further destruction of children. We must work for the elimination of social and educational practices which promote the welfare of some to the detriment and harm of others. Thus will we advance on the Commissioner's *Target for the 70's*—The right to read, the right to life, the right to love!*

—Matt Trippe

*This is a revision of the Presidential Address delivered by Dr. Trippe, University of Michigan, entitled *Love of Life, Love of Truth, Love of Others,* Annual Meeting, Council for Children with Behavioral Disorders, a division of the Council for Exceptional Children, Gary, Indiana, April 20, 1970.

Pain in School

Pain in school is

sometimes hiding from a harsh reality

Names whissspurred until they echo
    again, again, again, again. . . . .
    Until they fly aiming at me
      to hurt to *stop*

They *hurl* them at me
They *point* them at me
They *spy*   at me
   And they expect
     and expect
        and expect   me.

They are *too big*
I'm *not* too small!
Cannot—*they* see
   Will not—*me*
Can—*they* see
   Choose to—*me*
They can *not* see.....they stare
   blinding, hot like the sun
     I need the shade
                for
   sometimes, a few times, not many times. . .

    I do try
      I do
   from everywhere
my toes
my feet
my arms
my head
my hands
   every part of me *is* trying

They can *not* see. . .they stare
   blinding, hot like the sun

I need the shade.

3

Pain in school is

losing an area of expertise

I entered a Catholic school in the sixth grade with slovenly ways, but proud of my writing ability and spelling, with which I soon passed the other kids in the class.

Imagine the shock, though, the first time I went to the board to diagram a sentence, and the class and the teacher burst out laughing. It seemed I formed my letters wrong, and I had to be converted over to God's way of writing the English language.

Pain in school is

having an indifferent teacher

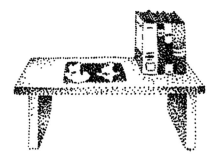

My unhappy experience was when I was—well—just last year. I worked on a project for about two weeks 'cause my parents didn't think I was doing enough extra projects for school. So, they wanted me to do one. So I did it. Then, when I brought it to school (these were the last few days) my teacher told me that—well—she didn't really tell me—but she didn't pay very much attention to my project. I made a map. And it just sat in the back of the room for a few days and I finally brought it home. I never got a grade on it, or anything.

7

Pain in school is

being fearful

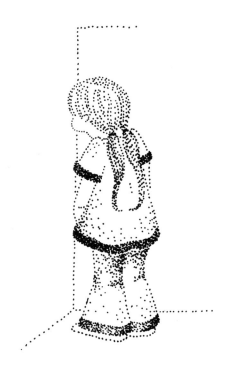

At six years, I attended first grade in a city public school system. My teacher was elderly. I was very shy and extremely intimidated by adults. I, therefore, remained quiet and docile in the classroom. One day while my reading group was exhibiting their skills in the front of the room my teacher was called out. While she was gone my girlfriend dared me to lean over and kiss my special but secret boyfriend. Gathering up my courage I did just as she requested which caused some giggling and excitement. To my dismay my teacher had witnessed what I soon learned was a crime. I was immediately reprimanded and sent to the cloakroom to stand in the corner because I couldn't "conduct myself as a lady." Crying my eyes out and trembling with fear, I spent at least ten years (ten minutes?) in that dark dungeon; this however was not punishment enough! Gym class was next and my gym shoes were perched on top of a cabinet. Being the giant I am, I was unable to reach them unassisted. My fear and humiliation prevented me from asking the teacher for help. I stood alone after everyone had left until the teacher discovered me, convinced me to tell her why I wasn't in gym class, and finally handed me my tennis shoes sending me on my way. I will never forget how unjustly I was treated for an innocent act of affection and how powerless I was to defend myself.

Pain in school is

having to experience
physical punishment

My worst experience in school was when I got this real mean teacher in sixth grade. Boy, every time you did something wrong, he'd go out in the hall and get the paddle. And then after that, you'd get sent to the principal and get the paddle from him too. Boy!

Pain in school is

being exposed to a violent teacher

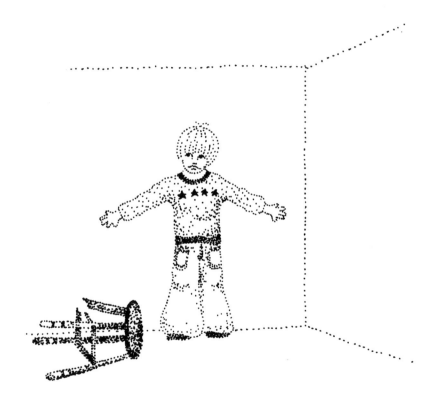

The saddest experience of my school years was when I was working on an operetta called "Rip Van Winkle." Someone was goofing off, so our teacher, who is quite a violent man, picked up a stool and threw it halfway across the room. The thing busted in half just about over a person's head— which scared me quite a bit.

Pain in school is

experiencing shame

When I was in the sixth grade I was taking violin lessons from the school music teacher. One afternoon, just as school was getting out and we were lining up to go home, he burst into the classroom looking ruffled and displeased. He spoke to my history teacher, alone, but in a voice easily heard by those nearby. In an overdrawn imitation of my mother he said, "Joanne is upset and unhappy about her violin lessons. What can be done about it??????????" And he went on, "What am I supposed to do about her daughter? What does she think I can do?" etc., etc. My violin teacher did not know that I was in the room. He seemed to have forgotten that we kids were there and could hear his words and see how upset he was. Instantly, I knew that my mother had been there and that he had not appreciated the visit. I was frozen with shame and fear. I knew that my mother came out of love and concern for me and that she was a gentle, courteous, and educated person (herself a former teacher). I knew that she would not have given offense. I was terribly upset by his reaction to her visit. He said no more. We children left for home. None of my classmates mentioned the incident to me. But I was hurt. I think that it bothered me most that he would make fun of my mother and especially in public. My strongest emotion must have been shame.

Pain in school is

learning not to be yourself

Being in first grade meant a lot to me since I had looked forward to going to "real" school, not kindergarten.

My first morning, our teacher took us through a singing lesson. I loved to sing, so I really opened up. After a minute or so of this, she stopped us, turned to me—right in front of the class—and said, "Stop singing at once! Your notes are all wrong and you are so much louder than the rest of the class."

It was just a thoughtless act, but when I went home that afternoon, I cried and told my mother all about it.

Pain in school is

learning to feel embarrassed

While in the second grade a question was asked and I raised my hand with much anticipation because I knew the answer and I was the only one who had any idea of the correct answer.

I was wrong and the teacher proceeded to tell me how dumb I was to think that I could do better than her more well-versed students. This tirade went on for about ten minutes while she told me to go to the head of the class and talk about why I had made such a "stupid" answer. At the end of this she told me my zipper was down which gave me much more embarrassment.

Pain in school is

traveling a lonely road with a hurt
that takes many years to heal

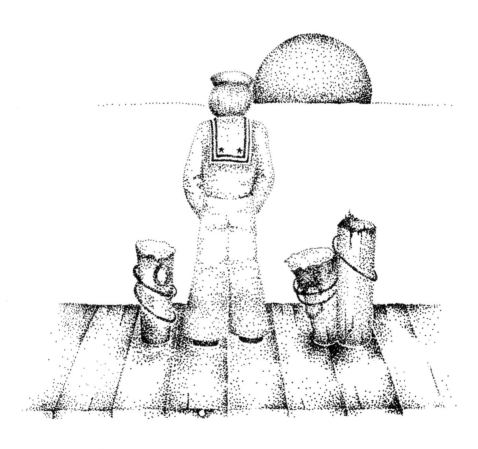

"I am sure you will be better off in the service. The service can teach you a trade. Maybe you can finish high school while in the service."

Seventeen years old and my world had just completely collapsed around me. I had just been told by my counselor that I would be better off in the service than in school.

He was polite, very sympathetic but he was still saying, "Sorry, boy, you are too dumb for school!" Even today I would like to tell him to stick his advice in his ear! My work in school had not been good, but I felt much of that was due to the fact I did more playing than studying.

When I left school that day I wondered what I would tell my parents. What could I tell myself? How could I fight a gnawing, cancerous emotion of worthlessness? I wondered how I could face my buddies. I remember having an over-whelming urge to run, to hide, to get away. But, where does a seventeen-year-old boy hide? The only hiding place I could find was the service. That day, I enlisted in the Navy before I went home. There was only one paper to be signed before I left for the service, that was a parental permission paper for men under eighteen years of age—they signed!

The hurt I felt that day almost twelve years ago has actually helped me today. When I am working with a boy who is called stupid, can't read, maybe he feels like he isn't worth much. I can go a little further than just sympathizing with him, I can feel what he feels...

Some refer to such feeling as sensitivity. Call it what you will, but I can simply tell my students to "move over, brother, you have company. I've been down this road before once by myself. It's a lonely road, let me travel with you."

Pain in school is

suffering the consequences of competition

The saddest thing that happened to me was when we had a spelldown and I couldn't become one of the people who went to another place.

Pain in school is

having your feelings ignored

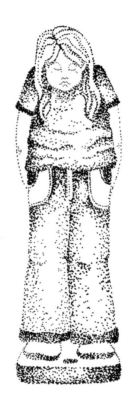

In thinking back to those "magic years" my focus came quickly to the year 1949, and the experience as vivid and painful as if it happened yesterday.

The experience was set in motion with the teacher's announcement that she was asked to weigh and measure the height of each student for the school records. Being heads taller and many pounds heavier than any child in the class (boys included) and extremely sensitive about my Amazon stature (my parents often made reference to this fact) my first reaction was no less than panic. All I could think of was running, running anywhere to escape from the scales; a dream I was to have for several years after this time on many occasions.

As each child was called alphabetically to the front of the room to have his weight and height charted on the blackboard (for all the *world* to see) my panic grew. When my name was finally called, I began walking slowly to the front of the room and as I passed the door I suddenly and seemingly without plan darted out the door and ran to the nearest available hiding place, the girls' restroom, where I found sanctuary for what seemed like hours until the teacher bodily dragged me out. As I attempted to explain my "unruly behavior" she "would have none of this nonsense." So back we "marched" and up went *Judy, 110 lbs., 5'3"* as bold and degrading to me as life itself seemed that day. I remember looking at it again and again that day and thinking that she might as well have put it in big red letters, for it appeared to jump out at you in contrast to all the others.

With no further attempt to discuss the matter, the teacher announced in front of the class that I would have to stay in during recess and write one hundred times, "I must not leave the room without permission." A valuable lesson, no doubt, for the class to learn!

Pain in school is

having a teacher
who makes you feel insecure

When I was in my first year of elementary school, I was extremely shy to the point where I received a "B" in "Speaks Clearly" because I hardly spoke above a whisper when called on for an answer. I guess now that the teacher had the purpose in mind of bringing me out of my shell when she chose me to do a job for her during class. She told me to go around from desk to desk and look at the children's notebooks to see if the sentences they had just written were neat. She said if they were sloppy, I was to tear up the child's work. She told me that she was going to check the work when I was finished and if she found that I hadn't torn up all the poor work that she would tear up mine as a penalty for disobeying her. To this day, I can remember the names of the two children whose work I had torn up. To me this was not a way to solve a child's problem. From personal experience, I can vouch for the fact that it didn't give me any added sense of security as a member of the class. I not only felt insecure with the teacher at that point, but also the dimension of my insecurity had then come to envelop my relationship with my peers.

Pain in school is

having a teacher who uses you
to meet her own needs

My family moved during the summer before I entered fourth grade. I wasn't at all anxious about leaving my friends, but I was frightened to begin in a new school. The few friends I had made during the summer went to a Catholic school so I was completely alone on the first day. I will never forget my traumatic first day in the new school...

The teacher had put some dictionary words on the board, and she asked if anyone knew what the mark above the word was. We had learned what accent marks were in my old school, so I raised my hand. I was the only one who knew the answer, she was pleased, and this incident led to a tirade about how dumb everyone was and how ashamed they should be to have a new girl come in and show them up. I went home that day and cried for hours, and did the same for many days after that. I gradually adjusted and made friends, but I always felt uncomfortable in that class. She was un-believably cruel and critical of the others, and I was always "teacher's pet."

Pain in school is

living by rules that dehumanize

When I attended first grade it was in a beautiful new school only a couple of years old. However, it was 50 years ago so that meant there was one girls' and one boys' bathroom on the whole first floor which was the elementary floor.

I suppose, in order to "maintain discipline," we marched in straight, silent lines to the bathroom at certain specified times, whether we had to use the facilities or not. Of course, if you were so unfortunate as to have to go at any other time, you had to wait.

It was early in my first grade year, perhaps I was still used to the freedom of the bathroom at home and in the kindergarten, however, I had to go. I was refused permission... and wet my pants while waiting our turn to march down the hall. As if this was not embarrassing enough, I was ordered to the chalkboard to do an arithmetic problem. When the teacher noticed my damp dress she thundered across the whole room, "Stand in the hall!"

To have to stand in the hall in wet clothes was pretty awful for me since I was one of the "good kids" that *never* got in trouble. My punishment did not end there! Just about every teacher in that whole lower hall somehow passed by (and they all knew me) and managed to "tsk-tsk" or stop for a little chat about the virtues of being good in class or at least to say, "I never thought that *you* would be out here."

Even *that* would have been endurable but my minister walked into school. I adored that wonderful man, but when he also assumed that I must have been very bad. . .I sobbed. To this day I cannot understand how adults could be so uncaring of my feelings.

31

Pain in school is

feeling the teacher doesn't care

During elementary school I adjusted easily to the classroom situation and did not cause any real trouble for my teachers. However, in the fifth grade, I could sense that my teacher did not especially care for me. I sat in the back of the room (as all W's do—an emotional experience in itself!) and acted as a normal fifth grader. Of course, I wasn't perfect, and at times, my interest wandered to boys, outside activities, and the usual pastimes. One day, the teacher mentioned to the class that she did not approve of gum chewing in the classroom, and she asked me, specifically, to get rid of mine. This did not bother me; however, the next day she really got the best of me!

I have the habit of twisting my hair, often while I am studying or relaxing. I suppose this gives me a sense of security and something to do with my hands. In the fifth grade, I wore a ponytail usually in curls. On this particular day, the teacher stopped in the middle of her sentence and told me to stop twisting my ponytail, that it bothered her very much, and that I should not do it again! I was completely embarrassed, did my best not to cry, and wanted to crawl under my seat. She had hurt my feelings and my pride in front of my peers.

Pain in school is

experiencing personal conflict

During the spring of my junior year in high school, my English teacher, an elderly woman whom I respected and admired immensely, had assigned a number of books to be read and reported on orally during the school year. At the time, I was very busy in cheerleading, club groups, academic subjects, and a myriad of social activities. Although I was unaccustomed to cheating, on this occasion I decided to go that route as I did not have enough time to read the book to be reported on. I had seen the movie on the book many years before and quickly skimmed through the book searching for enough tidbits to fake my way through the report. My turn came. I "weaseled" through, dressed in my cheerleading uniform and all. After the comments, I asked for and received my grade which was somewhere between an A and a B. Feeling sheepish, but smug, I couldn't wait to tell my friends how well I thought I had done considering I hadn't read the book! I believe I made this comment as we were leaving the English class in the afternoon.

Before the scheduled pep rally, I found out somehow that my teacher had either overheard my comment or had been informed of it. At any rate, the teacher I owed so much to for having given me extra help in spelling and grammar, now knew I was a cheat. Worse than that even, because I was boasting of deceiving her. All during the pep rally, I felt sick. Here I stood, a representative of the school, a student to be respected, an outstanding citizen of the school!

Good or bad, I went to see my teacher after school that day. I explained how ashamed I was, particularly for making her look like the dupe. I was truly sorry, not just because I got caught.

I'm sure my apology was very necessary in assisting me to reestablish my fallen dignity. It perhaps may have affected her also as it implied that I really did care about the sensitivity of her feelings and also her opinion of me.

Pain in school is

making it through"in spite of" it all

"In spite of" seems to be an apt description of school education today for it seems that one succeeds in spite of his schooling if he has other advantages such as a middle class background... The outstanding attitude schools ingrained in me was the dichotomy between learning, which is work to be done in school, and play, which is fun to be experienced at other times in some other place. How many children swear that recess, lunch, or physical education are the best parts of school? I surely did. One of the few distinct pleasant memories I have of elementary school is my third grade class in which we played Around the World with arithmetic facts combining learning and play. Most schools have not really changed much in the last few years. I have a nine-year-old friend who wants to be a beautician because you don't have to go to college for that. Well, if learning is portrayed and perceived as work, it will continue to turn children off. Perhaps more than anything else school destroys a love or quest for learning.

I also remember the unfairness of school. You had to do something because the teacher or the principal said so. I remember being placed in an advanced math class in sixth grade based on some test we had taken. I could not do the work and ended up hating math. Or there were times when you would tell on someone and the teacher would reply that she did not like tattletales but when you were the offender it was in the corner or the hall to pay for your crime. And it went on like that from September to June year after year with an occasional bright spot.

I don't think many people look back upon their elementary school days as happy ones.

Joy in School

Joy in school is

mutual respect

My senior homeroom teacher and I had very different, if not opposite, approaches to almost everything. I respected and feared her to a degree and yet I challenged some of her opinions. Throughout the year, she had always given the impression of being angered by my statements and I used to wonder whether I should just shut up and leave her alone. Graduation night, she made a special effort to find me and she said, "I enjoyed having you in my class. I think we've both learned a lot from each other."

Joy in school is

sometimes never found

After much thought, I have finally found one experience which I can call joyful in my school years...

The first few minutes of the first day of school when I began first grade seems to be the first and last joyful school experience. Finally, I would be able to read, to write my own name, to learn to add and subtract like my brother, to meet and play with lots of other children. It was so great to walk with my mother into the classroom. Then, meeting the teacher and finding a desk of my own assured me that I was off on the thrilling adventure I was so sure school would be.

It's hard to describe that feeling of anticipation I felt. I wanted so much to be a participant in life. School I saw as my pathway to "growing up." My waiting had ended.

Joy in school is

having a sensitive teacher

The happiest thing that ever happened to me was when I was first coming into school. All the kids made fun of me and the teacher took me in and was kind to me.

Joy in school is

a teacher who provides you
with a feeling of inner strength

One school experience seems to have remained with me longer than all the rest. It happened near the end of second grade.

I had a teacher who praised me for knowing that w-i-n-d was *wind* as well as *wind* and being able to identify it in context.

My family moved at the end of that school year, but I thank Mr. K. for his kind words. I believe they helped make the rest of my school days pleasant because I had been given a sense of success.

Joy in school is

having a contagious teacher

My first taste of geography came in the fourth grade, and I didn't think much of it. I approached fifth grade geography with a fairly negative attitude, but the first few classes brought with them a pleasant surprise.

My teacher was really interested in the subject material. She knew what she was talking about and she was enthusiastic about introducing us to the subject.

I think it was as much my teacher as her methods of instruction that made fifth grade geography so enjoyable. She had a genuine concern for us as individuals as well as an interest in our academic growth, and she let us know it.

Joy in school is

having the courage to try something new

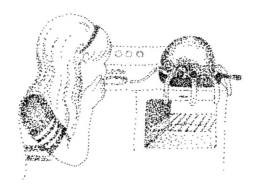

I was shown an octopus, laying dead in a pan—then it was cooked and served to us. I was the only kid in the class that would eat it. It was made into soup and was a brown cocoa color and very thick.

Joy in school is

having a principal who cares

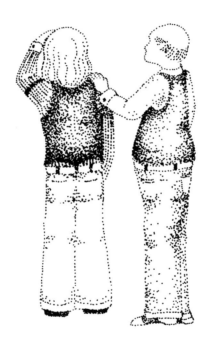

When I was a sophomore in high school, I tried out for the spring musical. I had a pretty good voice and was in the choir, so I thought I would get some sort of part. I *never* expected the lead! After many hours of practice, we put on two shows. I guess you really have to do it to know how it feels to perform in front of people who applaud for you, but it is an exuberant feeling of accomplishment and pride. After the show, people came backstage to congratulate us. I was taking off my wig when I felt someone's hand on my shoulder. It was the principal. The words he spoke to me that night are long forgotten. I just know that for some reason the fact that he would take time to come backstage and compliment my performance made the whole experience much more meaningful. It may have been a simple thing for him to do, but it meant very much to me. It was my most joyful school experience.

Joy in school is

sometimes feeling good
for the wrong reasons

When I was in kindergarten, there was this boy named Billy. Nobody liked him because he was a bully, a brat, and he was always wrecking other people's property. So at play-time we were playing with the giant blocks and I took one of them that was about the size of a 2x4 and hit him right on the head, and that really made me feel good. And I just got in a little bit of trouble.

Joy in school is

being a pioneer

My dearest friend Karen and I were chosen to be Patrol Girls. We were two of three hundred girls selected from throughout the United States. This was the first time that girls had been used for public school patrol work. As I recall, I felt very elated and proud to be a Patrol Girl. Patrol Boys were all highly respected by the student body and at this time I achieved this stature. As I look back, I see this as my first "Place-In-The-Sun" experience. It certainly must have been a great ego-builder.

Little did I realize at the time that I might be considered a pioneer in the Women's Liberation Movement!

57

Joy in school is

vowing to make things different

After considering my elementary school background, I am unable to name an exciting educational experience.

As a consequence of the teaching methods used and the general atmosphere of the Catholic school I attended, I feared and disliked every aspect of school. Emphasis was placed on strict obedience to rules and conformity to the teacher's attitudes. Learning was accomplished through memorization and word-for-word recitations. Questioning and presenting original ideas were considered disrespectful and were not tolerated. Examples were made of a child's failure, inadequacy, or disobedience. Physical punishment was enforced.

Consequently, creativity and reasoning ability were stifled. Fears and dislikes were established and school became a negative experience.

My elementary education, however, did have one positive effect. I am now aware of the importance of a child's self-image and of positive handling. I constantly strive to make learning enjoyable in my own classroom. Perhaps this realization, resulting from my elementary education, has been my most exciting educational experience.

Joy in school is

taking a bus into the real world

My happy experience was when I was young, in about kindergarten or first grade and I went on my first class trip to the zoo. And I was real excited! And I thought it was a real big thing, you know.

Joy in school is

finding a teacher
who turns you on to learning

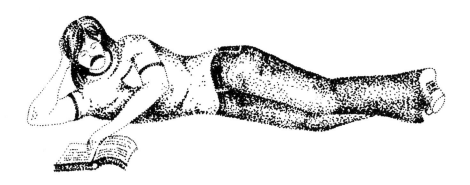

School was a competitive drag until my sophomore year in college. It is unfortunate that I cannot report one single joyous experience before that time, but there were none.

I registered for a modern drama course involving an intensive study of Chekhov, Strindberg, and Pirandello. A highly structured class, but the instructor was a brilliant, existentially-oriented lecturer. For some reason our minds and ideas "clicked." I *loved* Pirandello, did much extra work, and for the first time, experienced real communication on a cognitive level. Grades and/or the way others perceived my ideas were irrelevant—I was too involved in the discovery of my "intellectual" self.

This attitude transferred to many other courses—from genetics to Japanese literature. In fact, it changed my academic perspective. I acquired the capacity to enjoy learning.

Joy in school is

being missed

It had been a month and a half since I had been inside the school. I had been very sick with pneumonia.

Mom and I entered the tall red brick building and checked in with the school nurse. The old wooden stairs creaked as we climbed to the second floor. Whispers and cries of glee came from the corner fifth and sixth grade room.

My teacher met us at the door. The whole class clapped as we walked into the room. They were happy to see me and I was so glad to be back with my friends. The best part was the way they felt about having me back. It was beautiful to me.

Joy in school is

having your parents be interested

The best thing I liked in school was in kindergarten when you have these mats that you lay on for your naps. My dad drew a head on it and it told where your head and feet were. And the teacher really liked that!

Joy in school is

having a teacher who loves you

The happiest year of my life was in third grade.
Mrs. Jones was my teacher. I liked her very much because she
was in a way a nice and pretty lady who would understand
your problems and would try to help you with them. To
show her feeling for us, when we went to fourth grade, she
cried and kissed us all. It made me cry too.

About the Authors

Edward W. Schultz, Ph.D., received his degree from Syracuse University. He is currently Associate Professor of Special Education, University of Maine, Farmington.

Charles Heuchert, Ph.D., received his degree from the University of Michigan. He is currently an Associate Professor of Special Education at the University of Virginia, Charlottesville.

Susan M. Stampf, M.Ed., received her degree from the University of Illinois. She is currently a Resource Room teacher at Robeson School in Champaign, Illinois.